STRANGE SCIENCE AND EXPLOSIVE EXPERIMENTS

LUDICROUS
LIGHT

WRITTEN BY MIKE CLARK

PowerKiDS
press

Published in 2018 by
The Rosen Publishing Group, Inc.
29 East 21st Street, New York, NY 10010

Cataloging-in-Publication Data
Names: Clark, Mike.
Title: Ludicrous light / Mike Clark.
Description: New York : PowerKids Press, 2018. | Series: Strange
    science and explosive experiments | Includes index.
Identifiers: ISBN 9781538323663 (pbk.) | ISBN 9781538322703
    (library bound) | ISBN 9781538323670 (6 pack)
Subjects: LCSH: Light--Experiments--Juvenile literature.
Classification: LCC QC360.C53 2018 | DDC 535.078--dc23

Written by: Mike Clark
Edited by: Charlie Ogden
Designed by: Matt Rumbelow

Photo credits: Abbreviations: l-left, r-right, b-bottom, t-top, c-center, m-middle. Images are
courtesy of Shutterstock.com. With thanks to Getty Images, Thinkstock Photo and iStockphoto.
2 – Champiofoto. 4 – fboudrias. 5 – Vitaly Korovin. 6: l – Ivaschenko Roman; r – Happy Stock
Photo. 7: tr – Sashkin; bl – Sergey Uryadnikov. 8: l – H.Kan; r – Rob Hainer. 10: t – Studio
DMM Photography, Designs & Art; m – Winai Tepsuttinun; r – Esin Deniz. 11 – Alexandru
Nika. 12 – Bildagentur Zoonar GmbH. 13: t – s4svisuals; ttm – OZMedia3. tm – bezikus; bm –
Marc Bruxelle; bbm – Kostenko Maxim; b – Forest Run. 14 – Olga Popova. 15: bg – Dudarev
Mikhail; front – Brilliance stock. 16: tl – Arkadi Bulva; tcl – Shultay Baltaay; tcr – Scott Norris
Photography; tr – saknakorn; b – Paolo Gallo. 17 – amarrongelli. 19 – Balazs Kovacs Images.
21: t – Ruslan Ivantsov; b – Germain McDaniel. 22 – inxti. 23: Nathapol Kongseang. 26 –
Georgios Kollidas. 27 – Everett Historical. 28 – Morphart Creation. 29 – optimarc.

Manufactured in China

CPSIA Compliance Information: Batch BW18PK: For Further Information contact
Rosen Publishing, New York, New York at 1-800-237-9932.

CONTENTS

Page 4   **Light Laws**

Page 6   **Recoiling Reflections**

Page 8   **Cracking Colors**

Page 10   **Cryptic Coloring**

Page 12   **Wacky Wavelengths**

Page 14   **Radical Refraction**

Page 16   **Refracting Research**

Page 18   **Striking Speed**

Page 20   **Elusive Eyes**

Page 22   **Concocted Colors**

Page 24   **Eye Exhaustion**

Page 26   **Shocking Scientists**

Page 30   **Quick Quiz**

Page 31   **Glossary**

Page 32   **Index**

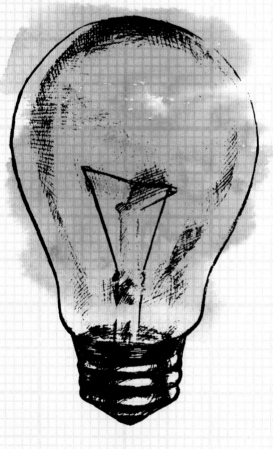

Words that appear like this can be found in the glossary on page 31.

Light Laws

Light is **emitted** by many sources. Some sources burn **substances**, which send energy out in the form of heat and light. This is how both the Sun and a fire make light, and heat. A light bulb is slightly different, as it uses electricity. This electricity is passed through a thin wire that gets very hot, which causes energy to be released in the form of heat and light.

Light allows us to see because our eyes **absorb** light to create an image. When a source of light is turned on, the light will travel out in straight lines, and then it will change direction when it hits objects. This means the light will bounce around the room. As the light bounces around the room, it changes from the color of the source of the light to the color of the object it hits. When the light bounces off an object into our eyes, we can **detect** the colors of the light.

Recoiling Reflections

One of the most important things to know about light is that it **reflects**. When light hits a surface, it will bounce off at the same angle. For example, look at the image here of light hitting a mirror. The angle labeled "a" is the same as the angle labeled "b." Light will always reflect off a surface at the same angle it hits an object. This is because light travels in straight lines.

Mirrors reflect an image of the room because they are made of smooth, shiny metal covered in glass. When light hits a mirror, all of it bounces off in nearly the exact same direction at the same angles.

a

b

Many objects do not reflect an image but still reflect light. For example, when light hits a tennis ball, the surface of the ball is not smooth like the mirror, it is rough. This makes the light reflect off the rough surface in many different directions. This is called **scattering**. The scattered light is broken up, so although you see the light coming back at you, you don't see a reflection, like you did in the mirror.

THE POLAR BEAR'S FUR IS ROUGH. THIS MEANS THE LIGHT SCATTERS WHEN IT HITS THE FUR.

Cracking Colors

Another important thing about light is that it can change color when it hits objects. But you will notice that it does not always change. When you shine a light onto a mirror, the light does not change color. This allows you to see a perfect reflection of yourself. However, when you shine a light at a shiny object that is colored, the light changes to the same color of the shiny object. For example, if you have a shiny red toaster, you will still see a reflection of yourself, but you will look red.

White light changes color because it is actually made up of many different colors. The different colors that we can see are red, orange, yellow, green, blue, indigo, and violet. All together, these colors create white light.

When light hits an object, some of these colors are absorbed and some are reflected. The colors that are reflected are the colors we see the object to be. For example, the tennis ball looks yellow because that's the only color it is reflecting.

BLACK SURFACE: NO LIGHT REFLECTED

WHITE SURFACE: ALL LIGHT REFLECTED

RED SURFACE: RED LIGHT REFLECTED

Cryptic Coloring

We can see the different colors creating white light together by making this cool spinning toy!

Step 1)

Use the ruler and pencil to divide the paper plate into 7 sections. Color the sections in the following order: red, orange, yellow, green, blue, indigo, and violet.

Step 2)

Use the pencil to poke two holes in the plate, each very close to the center. Thread the string through both holes and tie a knot so you have a big loop of string through the center of your plate.

Step 3)

Hold the ends of the loop, one in each hand, with the plate in the center. Wind up your spinner by getting someone else to turn it while you hold the string, or by flipping it over and over like a jump rope. When the string is really tightly wound, pull your hands apart and your plate will spin.

What Happened?

The plate should be spinning very fast – so fast that your eyes stop being able to see the different colors. Your eyes see white because they are seeing all the colors that make up light reflected at once!

Wacky Wavelengths

Although light travels in straight lines, it is made up of lots of different waves. Each of these waves is a different color. The reason different colors are absorbed by different objects is because different materials are capable of absorbing or reflecting different colored waves in light.

Light waves that go up and down very steeply are called high-frequency waves. Waves that are longer and shallower are called low-frequency waves. The distance between the same point on two waves is called a wavelength. High-frequency waves have short wavelengths, while low-frequency waves have long wavelengths.

There are many wavelengths of light we cannot see. This is because these waves have a wavelength that is too long or too short for our eyes to process. However, we know they exist because we have made machines that can detect them. For example, your radio set can detect radio waves! When the radio collects these waves, it turns the waves into sound that you can hear. These different waves sit on a scale called the electromagnetic spectrum. We can only see a small number of waves on the electromagnetic spectrum.

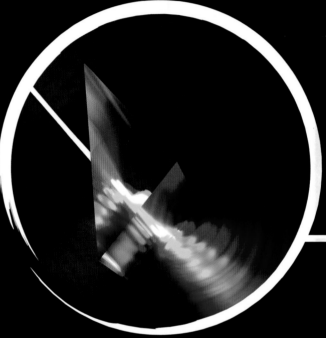

VISIBLE LIGHT

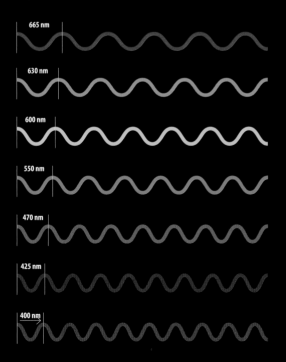

665 nm

630 nm

600 nm

550 nm

470 nm

425 nm

400 nm

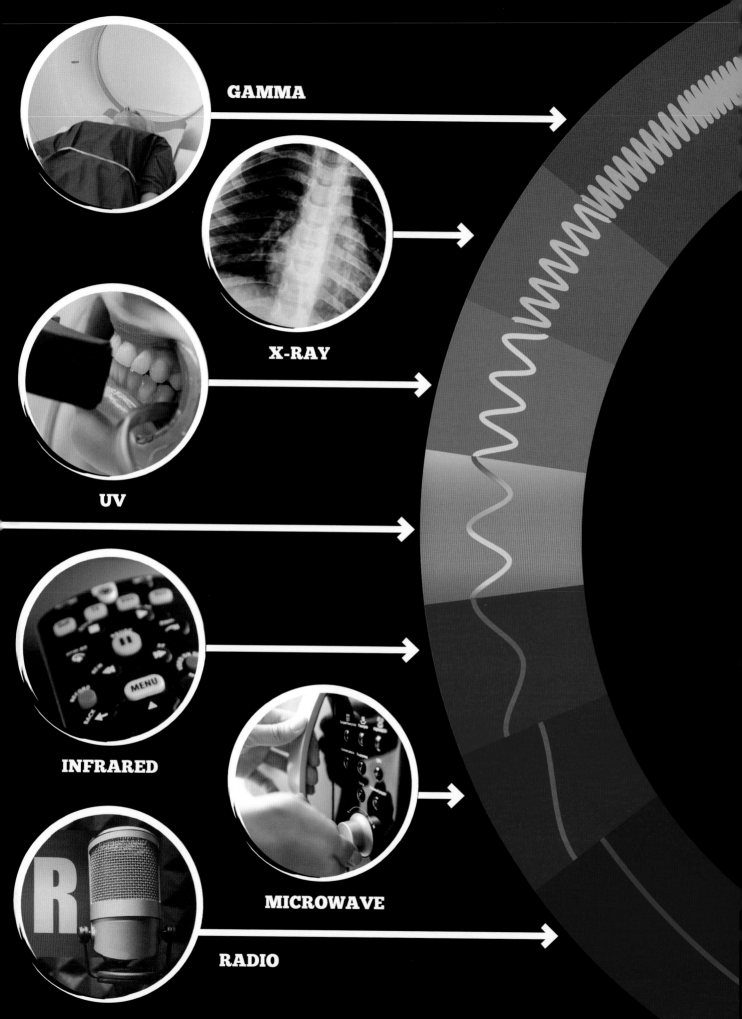

GAMMA

X-RAY

UV

INFRARED

MICROWAVE

RADIO

Radical Refraction

There are some objects that do not reflect most or all of the light that hits them. These objects are **transparent** objects like glass or water. When light hits water or glass, most of it does not get absorbed or reflected. Instead it will pass through them. However, light will bend as it goes through transparent objects. This is called refraction. Once the light has traveled through the transparent object, it will bend back again. You can see refraction happening when you place a straw into a glass of water. The straw will appear bent, but it isn't – it's just the light!

Light bends when it is slowed down. Water is thicker than air, which means that it is harder for light to pass through. Therefore, when the light hits the water, it is slowed down. As it slows down, the angle at which the light enters the water will change. The thicker the transparent object, the slower the light moves through it, which causes the angle to change even more. Glass, for example, is very thick and causes the light to bend more than water does.

WHEN YOU LOOK THROUGH WATER AT A FISH, IT WILL APPEAR CLOSER TO THE SURFACE OF THE WATER BECAUSE OF HOW THE LIGHT IS REFRACTED.

APPARENT
POSITION

ACTUAL
POSITION

Refracting Research

Refraction allows us to see all the colors light is made of. When light is refracted, the different wavelengths of color are also broken apart.

We can break light up into the different colors by using a CD, which will act like a prism.

YOU CAN TRY THIS YOURSELF. ALL YOU WILL NEED IS:

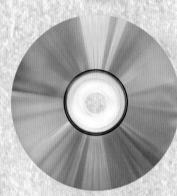

CD OR DVD

FLASHLIGHT

FAIRLY DARK ROOM

SHEET OF WHITE PAPER

Step 1)

In a dark room, hold your CD with the shiny surface pointed down at the paper.

Step 2)

Shine your flashlight on the surface of the CD. The CD will shine a curved line of different colors on the paper. Can you see the rainbow?

The reason the light breaks up is because each wavelength of light is bent at a different angle by the CD. Longer wavelengths bend less than shorter wavelengths. Red light has the longest wavelength and therefore bends the least, while violet light, which has the shortest wavelength, bends the most. This is why violet light is always on the inside curve of the CD.

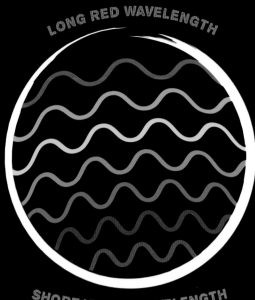

LONG RED WAVELENGTH

SHORT VIOLET WAVELENGTH

Striking Speed

Light is the fastest thing in the **universe**. The reason it is so fast is because it weighs absolutely nothing. This allows it to travel a distance of 186,282 miles (299,792 km) per second. This is so fast that if you could travel around the Earth in a car at the speed of light, it would only take you 0.13 seconds from start to finish.

Other waves, like sound waves for example, are much slower. They travel at 1,125 feet per second (343 m/s). This means that if you traveled around the Earth at the speed of sound, it would take you over 32 hours to get all the way around.

0.13 SECONDS

You can observe the difference in the speed of both light and sound during a thunder storm. When lightning strikes through the sky it will cause a loud rumble called thunder. However, even though both the thunder and lightning were created at the same time, you will hear the thunder a few seconds after you see the flash. This is because light travels much faster than sound.

Elusive Eyes

Our eyes can only actually pick up on three of the colors in visible light. These are red, green, and blue. This is because your eyes only have three types of color sensors, which are called cones.

To recognize the other colors, our brain has to do some work. Because the colors always go in the order red, orange, yellow, green, blue, indigo and violet, your brain can figure out if it is looking at the other colors.

If the red and green cones are both set off, then your brain knows it must be seeing a color in between red and green, which would be orange or yellow. If more green cones are set off than red cones, then your brain knows it is seeing yellow, but if more red cones are set off, then it must be orange.

RETINA

EYEBALL

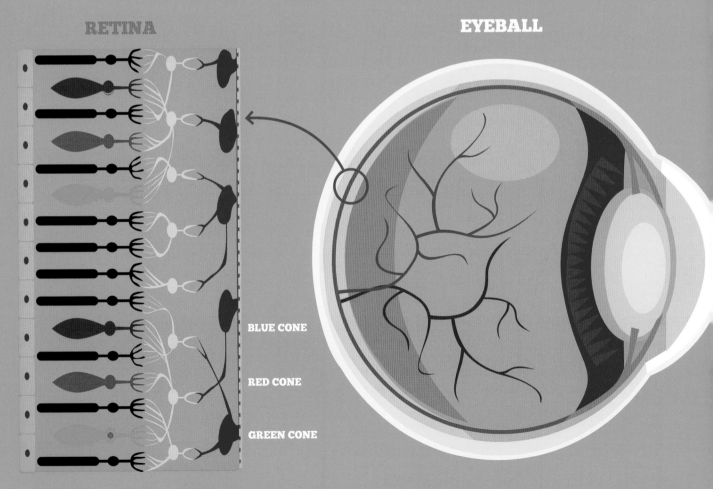

BLUE CONE

RED CONE

GREEN CONE

This is also how a television makes colored images. If you look very closely at your TV, you will see it is made up of lots of tiny **pixels**. Each of these pixels only has the colors red, green, and blue. To make yellow, your TV will simply show only the red and green lights in the pixel. When you are sitting far away, your brain believes that it is looking at yellow.

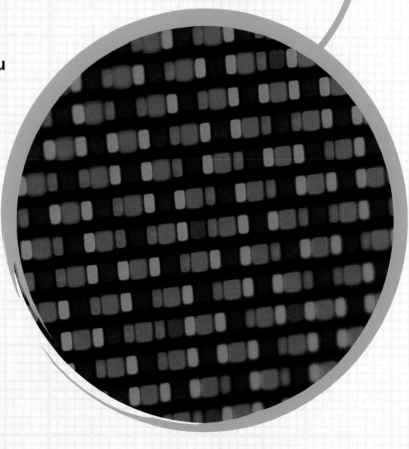

TV PIXELS

Concocted Colors

Not all the colors you see exist in real life. Pink and magenta are colors made up by your brain to fill a gap between red and violet. Color wheels show color changing slowly around a point, but this is not how the colors of light really work. Wavelengths of light do not circle back around to each other. Instead, the wavelengths just become too short after red and too long after violet, so we can no longer see them. This means that there are no pink or magenta wavelengths.

When the red and blue cones in your eyes are set off, your brain works out that it must be seeing a color between the two. However, there is no light wave of this color between the two, so your brain makes up the colors pink and magenta.

GREEN CONE

RED CONE

BLUE CONE

SPECTRUM OF VISIBLE LIGHT

Eye Exhaustion

Sometimes you will see colors that are not there when you look at something for too long. This is because when you look at an image for a very long time, the cones in your eyes quickly get **exhausted**. This will cause you to see weird, ghostly images. You can observe this effect with a quick experiment. All you need is a white sheet of paper.

Step 1)

Stare at the spot in the center of the weirdly colored British flag on the next page. Do this for at least 30 seconds.

Step 2)

Once 30 seconds are up, look at the white sheet of paper. You will see a ghostly image of the British flag, but even more bizarrely, it will no longer be in the wrong colors. The flag will now be red and blue.

The reason the flag changes color is because many of your green cones have become tired and have switched off. They will come back on eventually, but while they are off you will see color on the white paper. This is because the green cones are not sending any messages to the brain. Therefore, your brain assumes that there is no green light, and believes some of the light being reflected off the paper is blue and red, rather than white.

Shocking Scientists

Sir Isaac Newton

Date of Birth: Jan 4, 1643

Date of Death: Mar 31, 1727

Place of Birth: England

Hobbies: Poking his eye with pins and finding out what light is made from.

Sir Isaac Newton discovered that light was made up of different colors. Before this, scientists believed that light was simply white. They believed that color came from the amount of light, not the type of light. Newton proved this wrong when he managed to break up white light into its different colors.

Newton was also interested in how light behaved inside of his eye. In a disgusting and dangerous experiment, which could have blinded him, he stuck a pin into his eye socket and pushed his eyeball upwards. This changed the shape of his eyeball. By bending the shape of his eye, he could create colored circles, which proved that light was made of different colors. Don't try this at home!

Newton broke up the white light by passing light through a special glass object called a prism. The glass prism bends the light inside, so that when light passes through the prism, each color of light comes out at a different angle. Newton concluded that light was not white but in fact made up of seven colors: red, orange, yellow, green, blue, indigo, and violet.

NEWTON PERFORMING HIS EXPERIMENT WITH A GLASS PRISM

Christiaan Huygens

Date of Birth: Apr 14, 1629

Date of Death: July 8, 1695

Place of Birth: The Netherlands

Hobbies: Staring at the stars and investigating how light moved.

Light is very mysterious. Scientists to this day are not quite sure what light is made of, but they do know it moves as a wave. This was discovered by Christiaan Huygens with an elaborate experiment. This involved many screens positioned inside of a room.

Huygens placed one screen in front of a window, which had a small slot going down the center. This allowed light to shine through to the back wall.

If light was not a wave, it would only have lit up an area the same size as the slot it passed through. However, Huygens' experiment showed that light did not do this. Light moved through the slot like a wave and lit up a much bigger area of the back wall. When a wave moves through a small gap, the edges of the wave will curve and spread out. This is called diffraction.

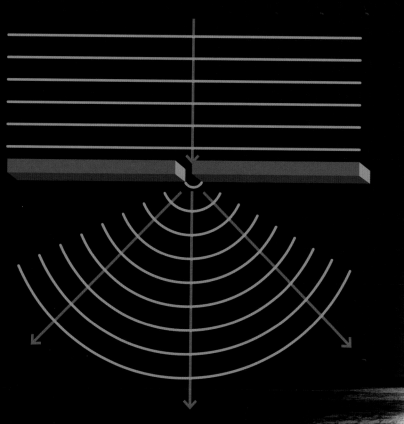

QUICK QUIZ

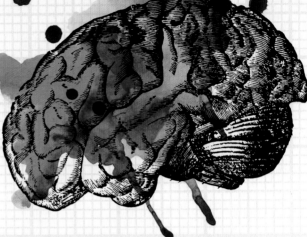

HAVE YOU TAKEN IT ALL IN? TAKE THIS QUICK QUIZ TO TEST YOUR KNOWLEDGE. THE ANSWERS ARE UPSIDE DOWN AT THE BOTTOM OF THE PAGE.

1. Name three sources of light.

2. What materials are mirrors made from?

3. How many colors make up white light and what are they?

4. What is the name of the spectrum of waves that light is a part of?

5. Is there anything that moves faster than the speed of light?

6. How long would it take to go around the world at the speed of light?

7. How many different color cones do you have in your eyes and what are they?

8. Which colors do we see that don't really exist?

9. What glass object did Sir Isaac Newton use to break up light into its different colors?

10. Who discovered that light acts as a wave?

GLOSSARY

absorb   to take in or soak up

detect   to discover or pick up on

elaborate   complicated or detailed

emitted   sent out or given off

exhausted   tired or worn out

materials   what something is made of

pixels   the small dots that together form an image
of a television or computer screen

prism   transparent objects with two nonparallel sides that
bend the light that goes through them

reflects   bounces back the light that shines on it

retina   the part of your eye that contains rods and cones

scattering   to separate widely and in all directions

sensors   something that responds to a physical
stimulus, such as light

substances   things with physical properties

transparent   a material that lets light pass through it,
causing it to be see-through

universe   all existing space and matter that
we know of

INDEX

absorption 5, 9, 12, 14

blue 9-10, 20-21, 23, 24, 27

color 5, 8-12, 16, 20-27

cones 20, 23-24

Earth 18

electromagnetic spectrum 12

energy 4

eyes 5, 11-12, 20-24, 26

fire 4

glass 6, 14, 27

green 9-10, 20-21, 23-24, 27

heat 4

Huygens, Christiaan 28-29

light bulbs 4

magenta 22, 23

mirror 6-8

Newton, Isaac 26-27

orange 9-10, 20, 17

pink 22-23

prism 16, 27

radio 12-13

red 8-13, 17, 20-24, 27

reflection 6-9, 11-12, 14, 24

refraction 14-16

rough 7

scattering 7

scientists 26, 28

smooth 6-7

sound 12, 18-19

speed 18-19

Sun 4

transparency 14

television 21

violet 9-10, 17, 20, 22, 27

water 14-15

waves 12, 16-18, 22, 28, 29

yellow 9-10, 20-21, 27